THE

VIRTUOUS

GIRL

THE VIRTUOUS GIRL

by
Danita Evangeline Whyte
with
Danae` Mary Louise, Daniqua
Grace & Danyelle Elizabeth Whyte

THE VIRTUOUS GIRL

Cover Design by Daniella Whyte & Daniel Whyte IV
WHYTEHOUSE DESIGNS, LTD.

© Copyright 2006
TORCH LEGACY PUBLICATIONS, DALLAS, TEXAS;
ATLANTA, GEORGIA; BROOKLYN, NEW YORK

First Printing, 2006

The Bible quotations in this volume are from the King James Version of the Bible.

The name TORCH LEGACY PUBLICATIONS and its logo are registered as a trademark in the U.S. patent office.

ISBN: 0-9785333-1-3

Printed in the USA.

DEDICATION

I dedicate this book to God, Who put in my heart to write this book.

And to my great and wise father, who taught me a lot of good and right things, and who led me to the Lord when I was seven years old.

And to my sisters who helped me with this book, and to all the young girls in America and around the world who I hope will get saved.

May God Bless You All Greatly!!!

The Virtuous Girl

Contents

ACKNOWLEDGEMENTS

First, I would like to thank my father for all he has done for me, and for inspiring me to write this book.

I would also like to thank my older sister, Danni, for being a good, big sister, a good example, and for proofreading this book.

A special thank you goes to my three sisters: Danae`, Daniqua, and Danyelle, for helping me to write this book, for giving ideas, and for being my best friends.

Also, I would like to thank my mother for proofreading this book.

And I would like to thank my two brothers: Daniel and Danyel Ezekiel for proofreading and doing the cover.

Lots of Love!
Thank You!

Foreword

I am very happy and proud to share with you that the book that you hold in your hands was written by my four youngest daughters: Danita (the main author), Danae`, Daniqua, and Danyelle. I am happy and proud, not only because they wrote the book, but I know, even though they are not perfect children, they strive to live by the virtuous principles that they write about in this book.

If you want a book written by young girls for young girls, that would help them strive to live the good life and also be more of a blessing to you as a parent, then I highly recommend this little book for you and them.

May the Lord bless you.

—Daniel Whyte III
The authors' Papa

*Special Note: I know that it will be hard to believe, but my wife, Meriqua, and I did not have anything to do with the writing of this book. Our four youngest daughters wrote this book all by themselves. All we did was proofread the book after it was written. We are just as surprised at how good the book is, as you will be.

Introduction

I was eight years old, going on nine, when I started to write this book. I wrote this book so that it could help a lot of young girls become virtuous, Christian, loving girls and young ladies.

You can become a virtuous girl at a young age. I decided to start being a virtuous girl, one day when I had done something wrong and I got chastised for it. After I got chastised, I had a bad attitude about it and I snapped at my father when he had asked me to do something. I got chastised again.

Afterwards, I was in the bathroom and was thinking about what I had done, and I decided that it was no use to keep on being bad and having a bad attitude. I had done something wrong and had been chastised for it. I just might as well change it, and I did. When I came out I decided to write this book, and I do hope that it will help a lot of girls, just like me, to become virtuous girls and to grow up into virtuous ladies.

—Danita Whyte

Who Can Find
A Virtuous Girl?

Who can find a virtuous girl?
For her price is far above sugar and spice
and all that is nice.
The heart of her parents doeth safely
trust in her because she has never lied to
them.
She will be obedient and not disobedient all
the days of her life.
She seeketh thread and a needle and learns
to sew, and she learns to cook and bake as
well.
She loves to do things for her family, and
helps her little brothers and sisters.
She shares her cinnamon rolls with her
little sister.
She gets her allowance and spends it
wisely, and makes sure she gives some to
the Lord.
She goes exercising with her family, and
strengthens her body.
She makes sure she does her best in
school, and always finishes her homework
before she goes to bed.

She goes with her family, and helps the poor and needy.
She is not afraid of the snow because she has learned how to make warm clothes.
She also makes herself beautiful clothes; her clothing is good and soft.
She welcomes her dad back home when he comes from work.
She makes fine clothes and gives it to the poor and homeless.
Happiness and praise are her clothing, and she shall rejoice in time to come.
She opens her mouth with wise things to say, and in her tongue is a kind word.
She looks beautiful no matter what, and tries not to do anything bad.
Her parents rise up and praise her,
And her brothers and sisters love her.
When she gets married her daughters will be virtuous too, and she will excel in all she does.
Foolishness is bad, and beauty is vain, but a girl that loves the Lord she shall be praised.
Give her of the fruit of her hands and let her own works praise her in the gates.

by Danita Whyte with my Papa,
(Daniel Whyte III)

Get Saved

Chapter 1

God is a very loving, forgiving, and merciful God, and He wants every single person to accept Him as their Saviour and come and live with Him, in Heaven, forever when they die. But, sadly, a lot of people won't because they don't accept Jesus Christ, God's Son, into their hearts and lives.

Jesus Christ came down to earth in the form of a man and died on the cross for your sins and mine, He was buried in the grave, and then He rose three days later, so that we could have salvation full and free. Jesus Christ loved us so much that even when many people didn't believe on Him, He still went through all the pain and suffering for them, and for us.

Jesus doesn't want anyone to go to Hell and be tortured there forever and ever. He loves everyone, and wants everyone to live with Him in Paradise. He wants you to receive Him as your Savior so that you can have everlasting life and live with Him in Paradise, as well.

You don't have to keep on searching and looking for happiness on earth; only Jesus can make you happy, and give you real peace. Jesus can fill your heart with His love and mercy. He can forgive you no matter what you have done and no matter what is going on in your life. He will forgive you always. Jesus is very loving and merciful, and that's why He died for you on the cross of Calvary.

Jesus is looking down at you from Heaven, with His hands wide open, wanting you to come to Him and open up your heart and receive Him as the Lord of your life. But He can't wait forever because soon it'll be too late and He's coming back one day to gather up all of His faithful children and bring them up with Him into Heaven, where they can live in peace and security forever and ever. Jesus really, really, really wants you to be His precious child so that you can experience His forgiveness and live with Him forever in Heaven.

Jesus Christ, God's Holy and only Son, did a lot just for you because He loves you more than you or anyone else could ever love you, and He cares for you. Please accept Him right now, today.

Here's How:

1. Believe that God loves you more than anyone could ever love you. *"For God so loved the world, that He gave His Only Begotten Son, that whosoever believeth in Him should not perish but have everlasting life"*(John 3:16).

2. Accept the fact that you have sinned and broken God's law.

3. Believe that because of your sins, you are on the road to Hell, and that you cannot do anything to save yourself.

4. Believe that Jesus Christ died on the cross for your sins, was buried, and rose again.

If you believe the four things above, please pray this prayer:

> Dear Lord, I realize that I am a sinner, Please, please forgive me of all of my sins. I now believe with all of my heart that Jesus Christ was crucified, was buried, and rose again. Please come into my heart and save my soul and change my life. Help me to become a virtuous girl and do Your will. Amen.

Now you can have real joy and peace through Christ, start a fresh and anew and do His will.

See ya' in Heaven!

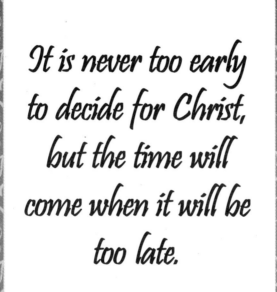

It is never too early
to decide for Christ,
but the time will
come when it will be
too late.

Pray and Read the Bible Daily

Chapter 2

Praying and reading the Bible is very important once you have become a Christian. Pray one time in the morning before you start your day, one time at night before you go to sleep and at least five times in between.

Reading the Bible should be fun. Read at least three chapters or more a day. You can do it different ways: read all three in the morning; all three at night; or one in the morning, one in the afternoon, and one at night.

Memorizing verses out of the Bible is important also. Don't just read it straight through and not do what it says. The Bible says: *"But be ye doers of the word, and not hearers only, deceiving your own selves"* (James 3:16). Don't just read three chapters straight through and then get right up and not do what it says and not remember anything you just read.

Memorize one verse a week or at least two verses

a month, and obey them because really the Bible is just God telling you what you need to do. If you read your Bible you will get more understanding about life and how you are supposed to behave. The Bible is your road map of life, and it's the best Book in the world.

It is important to pray because your life will go a lot smoother. Also, pray because God said not to worry about anything but to give everything over to Him in prayer.

If you have any problems in your life or you are not sure about something, pray to God about it and He will give you the answers that you need. It may not come right away, but it will come when God is ready.

Remember, God never sleeps; He is always and will always be watching over you, He will comfort you in your time of need, and He will always answer your prayers no matter how long it may seem.

So prayer is very important, pray a sincere prayer from your heart and ask God to forgive you of all of your sins, to give you strength for that day, and pray to Him also about your needs and wants.

Bible Girl!

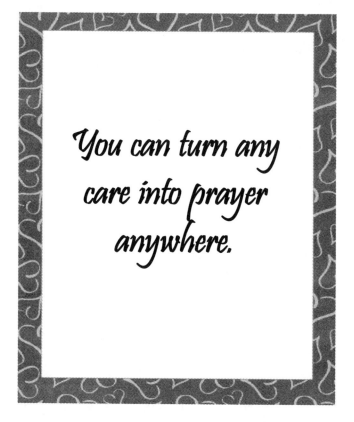

You can turn any
care into prayer
anywhere.

Go To Church

Chapter 3

Church should be the best place to you on earth. You should love going to church every Sunday and on Wednesday nights (if your church has Wednesday night services). Don't wish you could have stayed home and played sick. No, instead wear your best Sunday dress, put on your best sunny smile, and go to church to worship God.

Do not go to church just because your parents said to go, but rather go to church because you love God and you want to worship Him and do His will. Church is not a time for playing and talking with friends but a time to worship God and reverence Him and His Son, Jesus Christ. It's a time for you to pray to God and to praise Him for everything that He has done for you. Worship God in His House.

Church Girl!

If God stays at your
house during the
week, you ought to
visit his house on
Sunday.

Lead Other Girls
To The Lord

Chapter 4

Once you have accepted Christ as your Saviour it is very important that you lead other girls to the Lord. If you have peace and joy from accepting Jesus as your Saviour then God wants you to share that same peace and joy with other girls.

A great way to serve the Lord is by witnessing and leading other girls to the Lord. Before you can do that you have to make sure that you are living the way that God wants you to live. If the other girls don't see Christ's love in you and you are miserable, mean, and unkind to them, then they are not going to want to accept Christ as their Saviour.

If you are too shy or don't know how to approach them just give them a tract and pray that the Lord will touch their hearts to accept Him. Also, before you go out to go soul winning, ask God to help you and give you the patience and love to win other girls to Him, Also, ask Him to soften other girls' hearts to accept Him as their Saviour.

Don't give up if some girls keep on saying that they don't need Jesus and all of that kind of stuff. Keep on trying patiently and lovingly to win them to Him. Don't bug them a lot about it because they might bring it up themselves one day.

As a Christian, it is very important that you witness to other girls. When you are with Jesus in Heaven, and you see all of the other girls that you have won to Him, you will certainly be glad that you did!

"And He said unto them, go ye into all the world and preach the gospel to every creature. He that believeth and is baptized shall be saved; but he that believeth not shall be damned."
—Mark 16:15 – 16

God's Speed, Indeed!

(She) who lives like
Christ wins (girls)
to Christ.

Stay In School

Chapter 5

School is very important. Of course, it may seem hard going to school and studying Monday through Friday, but it will pay off when you are older, and you have a good paying job like a secretary, or you are an executive at Bank of America, or you're even the president of your own company.

Don't play hooky from school. Go to school to learn; don't go to school just to talk with your friends or to play outside at recess. School is not for that, school is for learning something new.

If math or any other subject is your weakest subject, don't think that you can't learn it. Try to learn it, and master it the best you can. Ask God for wisdom and understanding, and He will give it to you.

Try to make A's and 100's on all of your tests. When you make an 85% or above, treat yourself to your favorite snack or watching your favorite movie, but remember you'll never make good grades if you don't study.

Always pray — pray before every test or quiz or before you do anything at all. But you also have to study so that you will know that you know that you know.

Go to school to learn and come out knowing something new. Here are some good things to do and not to do in school:

- Sit up straight; don't slouch.
- Pay attention to the lesson.
- Write neatly.
- Don't cheat on tests.
- Don't pick on other kids.
- Don't chew gum in class.
- Don't pass notes in class.
- If your teacher is doing a good job tell him or her so.
- Go to school with a mind to learn something new.

Also, don't get too puffed up if you are the smartest kid in class, remember you prayed to God and He helped you, so it's not like you did it all by yourself. Still be humble. If one of your friends asks can she study with you or can you teach her Algebra, don't give her a sassy answer like, "Why, so you can be smarter than me, you know that's the reason." Don't do that. Help her and study with her because you might even learn some thing new yourself.

"Wisdom is the principle thing; therefore get wisdom: and with all thy getting get understanding."

—Proverbs 4:7

Stay in school and do your best. And remember to study hard, and pray to God for help because school is too cool to drop out.

School Is Cool!

*School days can be
the happiest days of
your life...*

Study Hard

Chapter 6

*"And further, by these, my son, be admonished:
of making many books there is no end; and
much study is a weariness of the flesh."*
—Ecclesiastes 12:12

Studying is hard and sometimes it is boring, but
it's always worth it when you see a 100% on your
test or quiz. The Bible says that studying is a
weariness to the flesh, but it didn't say that
studying was evil or was a sin. Studying helps us
learn better. If we didn't study we wouldn't know
anything. Remember when you had to study
multiplication tables? If you didn't study them,
then you wouldn't do well on your test.

Make sure that when you are studying you have
peace and quiet. Don't have your T.V. or music on,
or any other things around you that might distract
you from your studies.

The best place to sit while studying is at your
desk, in your kitchen around your dining table, or
at the library. Always have good lighting — not
too bright or too dim. Remember to pray to God

that He would give you understanding, and that He would help you as you study.

Have a thirst for knowledge. If you are taking English or Literature classes and if in the class you don't finish your workbook in time, try to finish it in your spare time at home because God wants us to be thorough and finish what we start.

Be Studious!

The highest
knowledge is the
knowledge of God.

Read Good Books a Lot

Chapter 7

Reading is also another important tool in helping us learn. Abraham Lincoln, one of the greatest presidents this nation has ever had, taught himself by reading the Bible and other books.

The first Book that we should read and master is the Bible. It is the most important Book in the world, and we can learn a whole lot from just reading it alone.

Only read books that are good and that will help you do good things. Reading bad books like Harry Potter can turn you away from God and make you start believing in witchcraft and all of that kind of stuff.

Reading has a powerful effect on the brain — good or bad. Reading good books on prayer and things like that can bring you closer to God. You don't have to read books like that all of the time. You can still read fun books like *Little Women*.

Reading is a good thing to do when you have nothing else to do. Just get one of your favorite books and read it. Reading can take you into a whole different world, and can make you dream and think beyond your wildest imaginations.

Reading is a lot of fun. Read to Understand.

Temples fall, statues decay, mausoleums perish, eloquent phrases declaimed are forgotten, but good books are immortal.

Know What You Want to Do and Be as You Get Older

Chapter 8

It's very important that you know what you want to do and be when you get older. The best time to start thinking about that is now — when you're young. To go out into this world when you are grown and not know what you want to do with your life is not very smart.

God put you here for a purpose, and that purpose is to do something that will please Him, and that will lead other people to Him. Pray about your life and your decisions to God, and pray that they will be pleasing in His sight. God might want you to become the next gospel singer, the next motivational lady speaker, the next missionary to China or Africa, or the next great movie star in Hollywood!

God has a purpose for everyone's life and we need to answer His call, whatever it might be. When you are about 9 or 10 years old you should start thinking and praying about what God would have you to do with your life. When you are in your teen years your decision should already be made or at least half-way made of what you want to do with your life.

If you feel God is calling you to be a missionary to Africa, Japan, China, or even to India start studying their languages, and start praying to God that He would prepare you for whatever hardships you will have to go through. By the way, if you want to be a missionary there will be some hardships to go through, but you won't think them so hard if you love the Lord Jesus with all of your heart and are doing it for Him.

Deciding young helps us when we become older so that we can start preparing for what God wants us to do, and also helps us to find out what classes to take in college. If our parents train us when we are young, as the Bible says, then we won't have any problems when we're grown.

Share what you want to do and be with your parents, because they can really help you make the right decision in what you want to be as you get older. Your parents know more about you, your talents, and your abilities, than you will ever know.

You only have one short life to live, so do whatever you can for Jesus Christ. Touch as many lives as you can while you are living, and making a decision right now about knowing what you want to do and be when you get older, can help you a lot and change your life forever.

Our purpose may not be to get a job at Dairy Queen. (But I'm glad for the people that work there, or else we wouldn't have any good banana splits!) It's about going all out for God, and doing the job that He has for our lives.

Remember, choose something that you truly love to do, because if you don't love it and you are only doing it half-heartedly, then you really aren't doing the purpose that God has for your life, and you also are not loving God with all of your heart, mind, soul, and spirit.

Maybe you haven't thought about what you want to be when you grow up yet, but it's never too late to start. So start now and remember to follow God's plan and will for your life in that decision and stick to it. God has a purpose for your life and He really wants you to fulfill it, and become the virtuous, Christian, loving girl and young lady that He wants you to be.

You Have A Purpose!

You can't plan for the future in the future – you have to start now!

Don't Lie

Chapter 9

Never, ever, ever lie. If you lie once, and then keep on lying, no one is going to believe and trust you with anything anymore.

Once my family had gotten a new car and my dad said not to tear it up or spill any drinks in it. I tore up a piece of the covering inside the car by accident. When my Dad asked about it, I told him that I had done it, and because I was honest and told him that I had done it, he did not chastise me for it, I just got hugs and kisses.

If you do something that your parents, your teacher, or anyone else, told you not to do, don't lie about it — tell the truth. Even if you do get chastised for it, they will still consider you a truth-teller and will respect you, and you will even feel better.

Lying is an abomination to the Lord, and He hates it. If you lie, and confess it, He will forgive you and forget it. The Bible says in Revelation 21:8: **"But the fearful and unbelieving, and the abominable, and murderers, and whoremongers, and sorcerers, and idolaters, and all LIARS** shall have their part in the lake, which burneth with fire and brimstone."

If you tell a lie, it's the devil telling you to lie, and if you yield to that temptation you are falling into the devil's trap.

If you took some cookies or candy without asking and your mother asks you about it, you might feel like lying and think that she'll never find out, but that's not the case. Your mother will find out and you will be in a worse situation than before.

If we really want to be good and do what Jesus says to do, we don't have to lie, because if we don't lie we will keep ourselves out of a lot of trouble. If you do lie, you might keep on lying, like David did in the Bible, until someone finds out and then you're in a big mess.

It's best to tell the truth any way, because Jesus and God are in Heaven watching over us and they know what we have done. Jesus had to go through a lot of pain for our sins, and Jesus is really sad when we disobey Him. We should try to be like Jesus, for the Bible says, *"be sure your sins* (that includes lying) *will find you out."*

The Truth Will Always Prevail!

58

It isn't right to lie
even about
the devil.

Do Not Have A Bad Attitude

Chapter 10

Bad attitudes and bad moods can turn a lot of people off from you; they are not going to want to be your friends or be around you. You will also be more successful if you have a good attitude, and you will benefit a lot more from it.

The only way to be happy and joyful, and not to be moody is to pray to God and ask Him to help you to stay on the right track and to have a consistently good attitude and spirit, no matter what. No matter how dreary or rainy your day may seem, still have a good attitude.

You can always wake up determined that no matter what, you are going to have a good attitude for that day. But, as soon as something goes wrong or doesn't go your way, then a bad attitude can come out again. That's why it's important to continue to pray to God and ask God for His help throughout that day, to control your temper, especially if you know that you have a problem with your attitude.

If something that you have been planning for a long time is cancelled, don't have a bad attitude just because of that little thing, something else great might happen that day.

If you have a bad attitude because something is troubling you, tell your parents. They can help you and give you good advice.

Here are some things that show you have a good attitude:

1. Obeying Your Parents
2. Loving Your Brothers and Sisters
3. Being Kind to Your Brothers and Sisters
4. Being Nice to Your Friends
5. Helping Out in Your Family

Attitude Matters!

If you are really concerned about what you wear, remember your facial expressions can be the most important.

Be Cheerful At All Times

Chapter 11

Always be cheerful no matter what happens. Everyone in this whole wide world has something to be happy about. As long as you are alive and well or even if you are alive and sick you should still be cheerful. If you have accepted Christ as your Saviour, and if you are at the point of dying or even if you are deeply wounded (like if you fell off your bike or something), still be happy because if you do die you will be going to a better place to live with Jesus Christ forever.

To be cheerful at all times, keep your mind and heart on Jesus Christ and only think on things that are good and pleasant. When you wake up in the morning, determine that you are going to be cheerful and joyful throughout that day no matter what happens. Whenever you feel yourself getting blue or you begin to feel sad, pray to God to help you to be happy, and to give you the strength for that day, and He will.

You will have troubles in life. Everyone does. But you still need to maintain a cheerful and joyful disposition. Jesus said in His Word:

"These things I have spoken unto you, that in me ye might have peace. In this world ye shall have tribulation: but be of good cheer; for I have over come the world."

—John 16:33

In this world you will have tribulations, troubles, and trials, but in Jesus Christ you will have peace.

The flesh does not want you to be happy — neither does the devil. They want you to be depressed and sad. But stand strong and be of good cheer for God has overcome this world.

Smile! It Can Make Your Day Brighter!

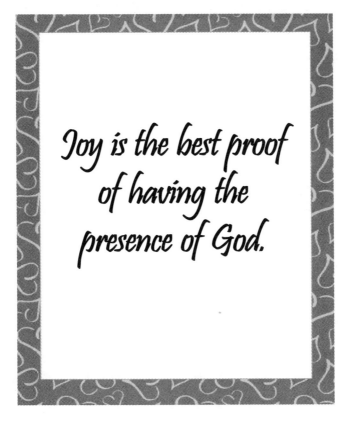

Joy is the best proof
of having the
presence of God.

Dress Modestly

Chapter 12

Dressing modestly is very important. God said in His Word that a woman should not wear men's clothing or a man, women's clothing. Even though there are a lot of cute jeans and other clothes out in the malls and stores, now, God doesn't want ladies and girls to wear them.

Ladies and girls originally wore dresses and skirts, and way back then it was really a disgrace for women to wear men's clothes. Today, that is not so. Now, there are jeans and pants for girls and ladies.

Even though unvirtuous clothes look pretty, there are still some skirts and dresses that are very nice, like the Bohemian skirt, which is very popular. Dress neatly and properly also. People will think more of you, if you dress modestly.

Dressing cleanly is also important. If you are going to school, going shopping, going to a movie, going to the beach, or even just staying home; still dress like something. Dress like you are serving Jesus, because if you are a true Christian you should be serving Christ even if it's just going to school.

69

Don't dress like a slob with stains on your clothes, ask your mom to wash them or you can wash them yourself.

Modest dressing is wearing skirts and dresses below your knees. As you get older always wear a brassiere under your clothes. Whenever you wear a dress or skirt that is see-through wear a slip. Slips today are hard to find because girls don't wear them a lot anymore, but if you really shop around you might be able to find some.

Look Your Best!

Your dress says it for you.

Obey and Respect your Parents

Chapter 13

Obey and respect your parents in everything. Even if you think that you should do something another way, still do it the way that your parents tell you to. You might slip and disobey them once or twice — everyone does — even us. But strive to be an obedient girl to your parents and for the Lord.

God said to honor and respect your parents in everything. Honoring your parents isn't saying "nope" or "yea" when they ask you something. Respecting your parents is saying "no ma'am," "yes ma'am," "no sir," and "yes sir." In the beginning, it may seem strange saying all of that to your parents, but it will get easier as you get used to it. Sometimes if you just keep saying words like "nope" and "yea," you might get used to saying it so much that, for example: the President of the United States may visit your school and ask you, "Do you like reading?" and all you say is "yea," that's not being respectful at all.

"Children, obey your parents in the Lord for this is right. Honor thy father and mother, which is the first commandment of promise that

it may be well with thee and thou may live long on the earth.

—**Ephesians 6:1-3**

Remember, still respect your elders and people who are older than you, even though they aren't your parents. Even if some people aren't older than you, still respect them. If you are walking past one of your friends, say "Excuse me." Be respectful.

Obey, respect, and honor your parents, and God will richly bless you and you shall have long life.

Promised!

A small step of obedience is a giant step to blessing.

Help Your Parents

Chapter 14

Always be ready to help your parents in any way you can. Your family should mean a lot to you. Many children don't realize how important and special their family is, and how they can be a help and blessing to their family.

Since your dad and mom work, and bring in money so that you can have a bike, scooter, nice bedroom, and a birthday bash every year, help them in return. Help by washing the dishes, helping to cook dinner, cleaning your room on your own, and helping with the laundry.

The reason why you should want to help your parents is because God wants you to, and you should want to do what is right.

Help your parents with things not just because I said it but do it out of your heart. If you don't do it that way then you'll have a bad attitude while doing it and the job will be done sloppily. If you do the job from your heart and you truly want to help, your parents will appreciate it, God will bless you, and you will feel a whole lot better that you are helping out.

Love your parents. When your parents come home from work give them a card telling them what you learned in school, what you want to talk to them about, and how much you appreciate what they do for you. After a long day's work your parents will appreciate that. Celebrate and plan for their birthdays, just like they do for you.

Helping and loving your parents is SUPER!!

Many hands make
light work.

Be Nice to Your Brothers and Sisters

Chapter 15

On my tenth birthday I got a jewelry set with a necklace and earrings, that I still have today. My sister Danae` asked me could she wear my necklace because we were getting ready to go to the movies and I said yes.

Be nice to all of your brothers and sisters, whether they are older than you or younger than you. No matter what, always be nice to them and love them. If they keep their room messy, help them clean it up. Maybe if you're kind and helping toward them, they might change and keep their room clean on their own.

If you don't love and be kind to your brothers and sisters here, God might take them away through a car accident or sickness. God didn't give you or me sisters and brothers for nothing. He gave them to us for playmates, to love them, and for them to be our best friends.

Help take care of your younger brothers and sisters. If your mom is busy, help her out by keeping them busy. Many other girls around this world and even in America want a little brother and/or little sister to love and take care of, but many of them do not have one. So thank God for your brothers and sisters, love them, and help take care of them.

Sister's Keepers!

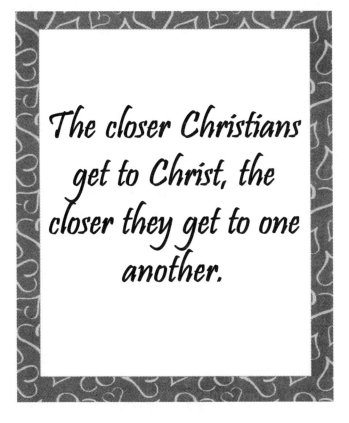

The closer Christians get to Christ, the closer they get to one another.

Take Care of Your Hair

Chapter 16

God gave each and every girl in this world her hair: long, short, curly, straight, nappy, black, brown, red, blonde, whatever. God gave you your hair to take care of and to love.

If your hair is thick and curly, be proud of that. "Be Happy Nappy!" Your hair is pretty because God made everyone pretty and every girl's hair is beautiful in His sight.

Perms are not bad; there is nothing bad about putting perms in your hair, but all girls don't need perms. If your hair is really thick and if your parents agree that you need a perm, then it's all right. If you don't need a perm in your hair, don't put it in just for style or just because your friend has it. Don't put a perm in when you're real young like 6, 7, or 8. Wait till you're a little older. If you put it in when you're too young or put it in too often, your hair could fall out or become short.

If your hair is curly or nappy, putting a straitening comb in it will work if you want your hair straight, but it's not the best thing to do. God gave you your curly hair, because remember, curly hair can go in some styles that straight hair can't go in and there are some styles that straight hair can go in that curly hair can't go in.

Don't cut your hair or trim your hair. God doesn't honor that, and, personally, we don't like to see women with baldheads or with hair that's real short. God said it is a dishonor for women to have no hair on their heads. If a lady has long hair it is a glory to her, not a shame.

Let your hair grow long, strong, and beautiful for God's glory!

There's only one beautiful head of hair in this world, and every girl has it.

Stay A Virgin

Chapter 17

A virgin girl is far more than sugar and spice and all that's nice.

If you want to be worth more than all the jewels and gold in the world, stay a virgin. Jesus wants you to stay a virgin because God wants to use you in a very special way. God used Mary in a very special way to give birth to His Son, Jesus Christ, and she was a virgin from birth.

Do not let a man or a boy touch you, kiss you, or hug you, and you don't touch, kiss, or hug a boy either. They can touch you in the wrong way and any thing can happen, like rape. Don't stare at a boy like you like him, and would like to talk to him. Just walk on by and go on to where you are going.

We don't believe in boyfriend/girlfriend stuff, and all of that doesn't just happen in your teen years; sometimes it can start in elementary school, when you're just nine or ten. If that happens you can really start getting messed up, thinking that you are older than you really are and start thinking that your parents are not allowing you to have the freedom that you think you really need, when they are just trying to protect you.

There is nothing wrong with sex, because God made sex, but there is something wrong with having sex before marriage. Only after you get married is it right to have sex. Just because your friend has a boyfriend and has given away her virginity doesn't mean that you have to do it, too. Save your virginity until you get married, if that's what God wants you to do.

Don't be concerned about what other girls are doing — looking at boys and being giggly. This whole world is caught up in that kind of stuff. There are very few virtuous girls and ladies in this world, so strive to be a virtuous girl and stand up as a model for other younger girls, and you might even be an example for older girls when you get older.

To stay away from looking at boys always stay occupied, always have something to do with you, because like the saying goes, "An idle mind is the devil's playground." If you are just sitting on the school bus going to school and you are just sitting there doing nothing by yourself, then a boy comes along and decides to sit there, both of you can start talking and getting to know each other very well. Then you can just start saying to your parents, "Hey, we're just friends, what's wrong with that? Every one's doing it."

Remember, God made boys to be more aggressive than girls, and they may try to talk to you, and get you to become their girlfriend, but that doesn't mean you have to yield to them. Even if you think that they are "cute," don't show that, no matter what you do. If you do that, then you've showed what you really think and feel about them and they know that they can get you easily.

Remember, you don't have to give your body away to anyone. God doesn't want you to do that. He wants to use you in a very special way for His Glory. If you give your body away before you are married you will feel cheated and you won't gain respect that way at all. Keep yourself pure.

True Love Waits!

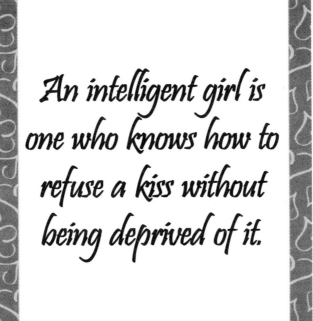

An intelligent girl is one who knows how to refuse a kiss without being deprived of it.

Be Strong, But Still Be Lady-Like

Chapter 18

This world is not as easy as a lot of kids think. You can't expect everyone, and everything to come to you as soon as you ask for it. You have to work for what you want, most of the time.

Being strong means, not breaking down at every little hurtful thing that comes your way. Being strong doesn't mean that you have to look mean and hard and be mean and hard. You can still be kind, loving, merciful, gentle, and strong at the same time.

If a food fight breaks out in your cafeteria at your school while eating lunch, being strong and still being lady-like means, if something hits you in your head don't throw something back at whoever threw it at you. That's not being strong or lady-like. Just get up and go tell the principal or the cafeteria monitor — that's being strong and lady-like. You know, being strong is not wanting to be a member of a gang when you get older — that's the wrong kind of strong. Actually being a part of a gang tears people down — physically and mentally.

Be tough-minded, no matter what other people say about it. If you believe that you can do something, and you believe that you have the strength to do it, you will succeed. Even if some roadblocks and problems come up, still persevere and get it done.

You should be nice and strong at the same time, because, if you are not like that, you can be too hard on people and things, and you can cause them to hate you.

Remember, be strong because God is with you and knowing that, you should have nothing to fear.

To Everything, Girl Power!

Courage is grace under pressure.

Love Yourself, How God Made You

Chapter 19

God made everyone unique, with their own personalities and makeups. You should love how God made you. You are really special in His sight and you are His creation. If you don't really believe this you can go into depressions, and think that you aren't as pretty or as slim as that girl you have on your poster in your bedroom.

Actually, some of the stuff that is on posters, in magazines, and on websites are totally fake. Some of those girls do not dress like that at home and they might not feel happy themselves at home. Just because they seem all happy on the picture, doesn't mean that they are like that at home.

Putting on makeup, jewelry, and fashionable clothes really won't change anything about how you look, because God sees your true self and you see your true self in the mirror everyday; even though many other people may not see that.

You have to accept the fact that God made you how you are, and you also have to accept the fact, that other girls might call you ugly names like "carrot head" and "fatty" and all of that. But don't worry about what they say. Think about what God thinks of you, and how happy He felt when He made you, and when you were born to your parents on your birthday.

All of these reality shows about "Extreme Makeover" are really crazy to us. Even though most people come out looking better; sometimes we think about how sad it makes God feel because people aren't happy with the way God made them, in His own Image — and that makes God so very sad.

Beauty — true beauty — doesn't come from the outside; it has to come from the inside — deep down from your heart. True beauty is all about love, kindness, being merciful, and being gentle. God doesn't look on the outside. He looks at the heart. If you don't look on your heart and understand how you really are then you can't love yourself, how God made you. I Samuel 16:7b says: ***"For man looketh on the outward appearance, but the Lord looketh on the heart."***

All the girls in your class may be pretty, and may become homecoming queens and beauty queens, but if you are the only one that has true beauty in your life, and you have accepted how you really are and you truly love how God made you; then in the end you will be the True Beauty Queen.

God loves you and Jesus Christ (His Son) loves you and they made you — wherever you are and whoever you are. He made you in His own image. So love yourself how God made you and be beautiful from the inside out.

Have High Self Esteem!

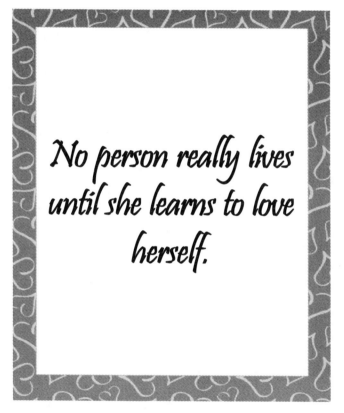

No person really lives
until she learns to love
herself.

How To Make Good Friends

Chapter 20

Your best friends should be your brothers and sisters that live with you, and that you see everyday. Create a special bond with them, talk with them, play with them, and spend time with them. They should be your "Best Friends."

As far as making friends outside of your home, just leave it in God's hands. There are a lot of kids out here in this world that can turn you away from God and get you into drugs and things. God doesn't want you to become friends with negative and bad people.

God will give you the right friends that He wants you to hang around with — friends that will stay with you through thick and thin, bad and good; friends that really love God and who really love you, and friends that are devoted to God. Those are the friends that God wants you to have and the friends that He will give you if you will just trust in Him and leave that up to Him.

Your number one friend should be Jesus. He will truly stay with you no matter what you will have to go through. Jesus said that He would *"never leave thee nor forsake thee,* "and that's a promise. Spend extra special time with your friend, Jesus, and talk with Him everyday through prayer and reading His Holy Word.

Good friends will tell you the truth, even if it might hurt you a little, but they are still your friends because you will know then that you can truly depend on them and trust them.

Tips For Having A Good Time With Your Friends:

1. Have Pretend Tea Parties Together
2. Play Together
3. Take A Lot of Pictures Together
4. Go To Movies and Parties Together
5. Act Out A Play For Your Families Together
6. Laugh A Lot
7. Have Your Birthday Parties Together

The way to make friends is to be friendly yourself. Be kind to everyone you meet. Be interested in what other people like to do. Some people are not going to be interested in you if you are not interested in what they want to do. Be concerned about other people before yourself, like Jesus did. I'm reminded of a verse in Philippians 2:4 that says, ***"Look not every man on his own things, but every man also on the things of others."***

Best Buds Forever!

Never choose friends
by their looks.

How to be Really Cute

Chapter 21

Every girl wants to be cute, right? Is real cuteness fancy clothes, makeup, jewelry, and high-heeled stilettos? No, real cuteness is being loving, kind, merciful, peaceful, understanding, and forgiving. When your heart is right on the inside and you are doing what's right, then you are truly being cute.

Your little brother comes into your room and messes up your books and CDs. Then you come in after him and shout, "No Kevin, you're always messing up things, get out of here."

Is that real cuteness?

No, it's not and it's not looking cute at all because when you shout and scream, you certainly don't look cute. Jesus doesn't care about all of the fashions on the outside, He cares about the heart. You can be the prettiest girl in your class, but if you are not pretty on the inside then you are not truly the cutest girl in your class.

Jewelry and makeup can make you look prettier than your true self, but that's only on the outside. You can't put makeup on your heart. You can't fake kindness for long, when for real you are mean.

Now, this is being really cute:

Your little brother comes into your room again and starts looking at one of your books or magazines, and he accidentally tears out one of your pages. Instead of shouting at him you say, "That's alright, Kevin, we can tape it up later, would you like me to color with you after I finish my school project?"

Now is that being really cute? It sure is.

Be cute, cool and collected!

Give your hands to serve and your hearts to love.

Be Faithful

Chapter 22

Be faithful unto death. Be faithful in everything. Be faithful! No matter what, be faithful.

If your parents give you a job to do, no matter how long it takes to do that job, be faithful and stick to it. It may seem that the job is just a little thing to do in your sight; but no matter how little it may seem, be faithful and stick to it. God said that He who is faithful in little things would be blessed with bigger and greater things in the future.

Be faithful to Jesus. Witnessing to others every chance you get is being faithful. Praying and reading the Bible everyday and going to church every Sunday is being faithful, also.

If kids are making fun of you at school just because you are a Christian and you are not going down the same path that they are, don't worry about that, be faithful to Jesus, and He will honor you for that, and other people will look up to you and respect you as well.

Jesus said that people would *"persecute you*

(Christians) *for my name sake but he* (or she) *who is faithful to the end shall receive a crown of life."*

"Fear none of those things which thou shalt suffer: behold, the devil shall cast some of you into prison, that ye may be tried; and ye shall have tribulation ten days: be thou faithful unto death, and I will give thee a crown of life."

—Revelation 2:10

Now, people won't put Christians in jail anymore, but some will make fun of you, and there are even some schools that won't let Christian kids do certain things. Once we read in the paper that a Christian girl was giving her speech in school at her graduation, and when she started speaking about Christ, they cut her microphone off.

Be faithful no matter what, even if it means dying for Christ because after all you will be going to a better place if you are saved. Being faithful pays off.

Faith Girlz!

It is better to be
faithful than to be
famous.

Be Committed and Consistent

Chapter 23

Be committed to Jesus so much that you have the attitude that no matter what, you're going to stay with Him, and serve Him until you die. Be so committed to Him that you cannot turn back from following Him, and that you always think about what Jesus would do if He were in the same situation that you were in.

Be consistent in telling others about Christ, how much He loves them and what He has done in your life. Be consistent in helping others who are less fortunate than you and be consistent in praying for others that need to be saved in America and around the world.

Work consistently on your schoolwork and most of all in your work for the Kingdom of God. God will reward and bless you for being committed and consistent to Him.

Some of God's most committed followers were ladies. Mary, Mary Magdalene, and Salome along with other ladies followed Jesus wherever He went. You can also be one of His committed followers and serve Him and follow Him forever and ever.

Also be committed to your family and friends. Be consistent with your jobs and chores at home, and always do them without having to be told.

Decide to become a committed soldier in God's Army, and you will win more than a purple heart. You will win a crown of life and live in Paradise forever.

I'm committed to Jesus!

The world crowns
success; God crowns
consistency.

Be Kind and Generous

Chapter 24

Be kind and generous to everyone. Even if a girl is real mean to you and tells jokes and plays mean pranks on you, still be nice to her. If you are still nice to her the time will come when she will change and be nice to you.

Be generous in giving to everyone, too. Give from your heart. Give without expecting anything in return. Be concerned about them. Many poor people die everyday, because richer people do not give to them, as they should. God said we will always have the homeless with us, so we need to help them as much as possible.

Also be kind to the people you see every day. Still say "please" and "thank you" — the magic words.

When we give unto other people, we're giving unto the Lord, and sometimes we can be *"entertaining angels unawares."*

Be kind and generous to everyone, the person that you help one day might become the President of the United States, when they are grown up. You will never know what a person is going through that day and your being kind to them could have just made their day!

Kindness Rules!

One of the strongest of
all virtues is kindness.

True Virtuousness

Chapter 25

Who can find a virtuous girl?
For her price is far above sugar
And spice and all that's nice...

A true virtuous girl is far more than all the jewels and gold in the world. She is priceless.

The heart of her parent's doeth
Safely trust in her, because she has
Never lied to them...

A true virtuous girl never lies to anyone about anything. Lying will just get you into a lot of trouble and no one will ever be able to trust you anymore. If you want your parents to safely trust in you never ever lie to them. A true virtuous girl wants to be trustworthy.

She will be obedient and not
Disobedient all the days of her life...

A true virtuous girl will always be obedient. She might disobey sometimes, but she will strive to be an obedient girl. Disobedience can cause you a lot of heartache, especially when you disobey God and your parents.

*She seeketh thread, and a needle
And learns to sew and she learns to
cook and bake as well...*

A true virtuous girl knows how to cook and bake goodies and is very creative.

*She loves to do things for her family,
And helps with her little brothers and sisters.
She shares her cinnamon rolls with her
little sister...*

A true virtuous girl loves to help her family and take care of and play with her brothers and sisters.

*She gets her allowance and spends
It wisely and makes sure she gives some
To the Lord...*

When a true virtuous girl gets her money, she always spends it wisely and never wastes any. She always gives her tithe to the Lord.

*She goes exercising with her family
And strengthens her body...*

A true virtuous girl always goes exercising and makes sure that she gets the proper exercise she needs and doesn't eat too much junk food.

She makes sure she does her best in
School, and always finishes her homework
Before she goes to bed...

A true virtuous girl always does her best in school, because she knows that it will pay off when she's older. Anyway school is too cool to drop out of.

She goes with her family and
Helps the poor and needy...

A true virtuous girl is very concerned about the poor and always wants to help them by giving them food, clothes, money, and the Gospel of Jesus Christ.

She is not afraid of the snow because
She has learned how to make warm clothes.
She also knows how to shop for beautiful
And warm clothes, her clothing is good and soft...

A true virtuous girl isn't afraid to go out in the winter — in the snow and cold because she can make warm clothes and can also buy them. She makes sure her clothes are clean, washed, and beautiful everyday.

She welcomes her Dad back home
When he comes home from work...

A true virtuous girl is always glad when her dad comes home from work and always welcomes him back.

She makes fine clothes and gives
It to the poor and homeless...

A true virtuous girl gives from the heart because she loves God and other people. She is very generous.

Happiness and praise are her clothing,
And she shall rejoice in time to come.
She opens her mouth with wise things
To say and in her tongue are kind words...

A true virtuous girl is always happy and cheerful and she never has anything mean to say. She always talks sensibly and nicely.

She always looks beautiful no matter what
And does not do any thing bad...

A true virtuous girl always looks beautiful and never dresses like a slob. She strives everyday to be more and more like Jesus.

Her parents rise up and praise her,
And her brothers and sisters love her...

A true virtuous girl will be praised by her parents because she helps them. Her brothers and sisters love her because she is always nice and kind to them.

When she gets married her daughters will
Be virtuous too, and she will excel in all she does...

A true virtuous girl, if God wants her to get married, will train her daughters in a virtuous way, too, and she will excel in all she does because she is serving God from her heart.

Foolishness is bad, and beauty is vain but a
Girl that praises the Lord she shall be praised.
Give her of the fruits of her hands and let
Her own works praise her in the gates.

A true virtuous girl knows that foolishness is bad and that beauty isn't the only thing that matters. If she praises and serves the Lord, she shall be praised.

No one can fake true virtuousness. If you want to truly become a virtuous girl follow God's path and will that He has for your life. Serve Him with your whole heart. And let Him make you into one of His true virtuous girls and Godly young ladies.

Girl For God!

A loving heart is the
truest wisdom

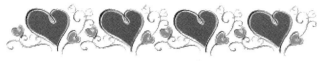

BIBLES

1. King James Version Holy Bible
2. A Faith To Grow On Bible — John MacArthur
3. Day by Day Kid's Bible — Karyn Henley
4. Wisdom & Grace Bible for Young Women of Color — Stephanie Moore

Inspirational/Helpful Books

1. Christian Girl's Guide To Being Your Best! — Katrina Cassel
2. The Christian Girl's Guide To Friendship! — Kathy Widenhouse
3. The Christian Girl's Guide to the Bible — Katrina Cassel
4. The Christian Girl's Guide to Your Mom — Marilyn C. Hilton
5. The Girl God Wants — Daniella Whyte
6. No Boys Allowed: Devotions For Girls — Kristi Hall with Jennifer Vogtlin
7. God and Me! Devotions for Girls
8. God's Wisdom for Little Girls — Elizabeth George

Fun Books

1. That's Not All I Found In The City — Sue Buchanan and Lynn Hodges
2. The Legend Of The Sand Dollar — Chris Auer
3. The Princess and The Kiss — Jennie Bishop
4. The Cul-de-Sac Kids Series — Beverly Lewis
5. Three Cousins Detective Club Series — Elspeth Campbell Murphy
6. Grandma's Attic Series —Arleta Richardson
7. Mandie Mysteries — Lois Gladys Leppard
8. The New Sugar Creek Gang Series — Pauline Hutchens Wilson and Sandy Dengler
9. Winnie the Horse Gentler Series — Dandi Daley Mackall
10. Young Women of Faith Series — Nancy Rue
11. Faithgirlz Series — Nancy Rue
12. Janette Oke's Classics for Girls — Janette Oke
13. Girls Only! (GO!) Series — Beverly Lewis
14. Accidental Detectives Series — Sigmund Brauwer
15. Left Behind: The Kids — Jerry B. Jenkins and Tim LaHaye

16. Keystone Stables Series — Marsha Hubler
17. Elsie Dinsmore: A Life of Faith Series — Martha Finley
18. The Chronicles Of Narnia Series — C.S. Lewis
19. Emily's Bracelet — Kandilyn Martin and Frank Martin
20. The Caroline Years Series — Maria D. Wilkes and Celia Wilkins
21. Little House On the Prairie Series — Laura Ingalls Wilder
22. Little Pilgrims Progress — Helen L. Taylor
23. Anne of Green Gables Series — L.M. Montgomery
24. Classic Pony and Horse Stories — Marguerite Henry
25. Building On The Rock Series — Joel R. Beeke and Diana Kleyn
26. Treasures of the Snow — Patricia St. John
27. Little Women — Louisa May Alcott

Fun Biographies and History Books

1. The Sowers Series Biographies — David Collins

2. Christian Heroes: Then and Now Series — Janet and Geoff Benge
3. New Heroes of the Faith Series
4. *Ten Girls Who Made History* — Irene Howat
5. *Ten Girls Who Made A Difference* — Irene Howat
6. *Ten Girls Who Changed the World* — Irene Howat
7. Sisters In Time Series
8. *American Girl History Mysteries*
9. Liberty Letters Series — Nancy LeSourd

D. V. D'S

1. The New Adventures of Black Beauty
2. Kingdom Under the Sea Series
3. Stephen's Test of Faith
4. Storykeepers DVD Collections
5. The Story of Jesus for Children
6. The Prince of Egypt
7. The Chronicles of Narnia
8. Left Behind

Videos

1. Christy Video Series
2. Testament: The Bible in Animation Video Series
3. Greatest Heroes and Legends of the Bible

Music C.D.'s

1. I Could Sing Of Your Love Forever: Kids
2. SuperStar Go Fish
3. Shout Praises! Kids 4
4. Crazy Praise Series
5. Songs 4 Worship Kids
6. Kids Scene Live Worship

Websites/ Fun and Helpful

1. www.thevirtuousgirl.org
2. thevirtuousgirl.blogspot.com
3. www.americangirl.com
4. www.clubhousejr.com
5. www.storybook.com